THE SAFARI SET

mibo®

Button
Books

MADELEINE ROGERS

Out on the savanna
the ground gets scorching hot.
The only place you'll want to be
is in a shady spot.

Lions are a lazy bunch and
sleep most of the day.

But when they're mad their scary roars
are heard from miles away.

The tall giraffes are rather good at reaching high-up leaves.

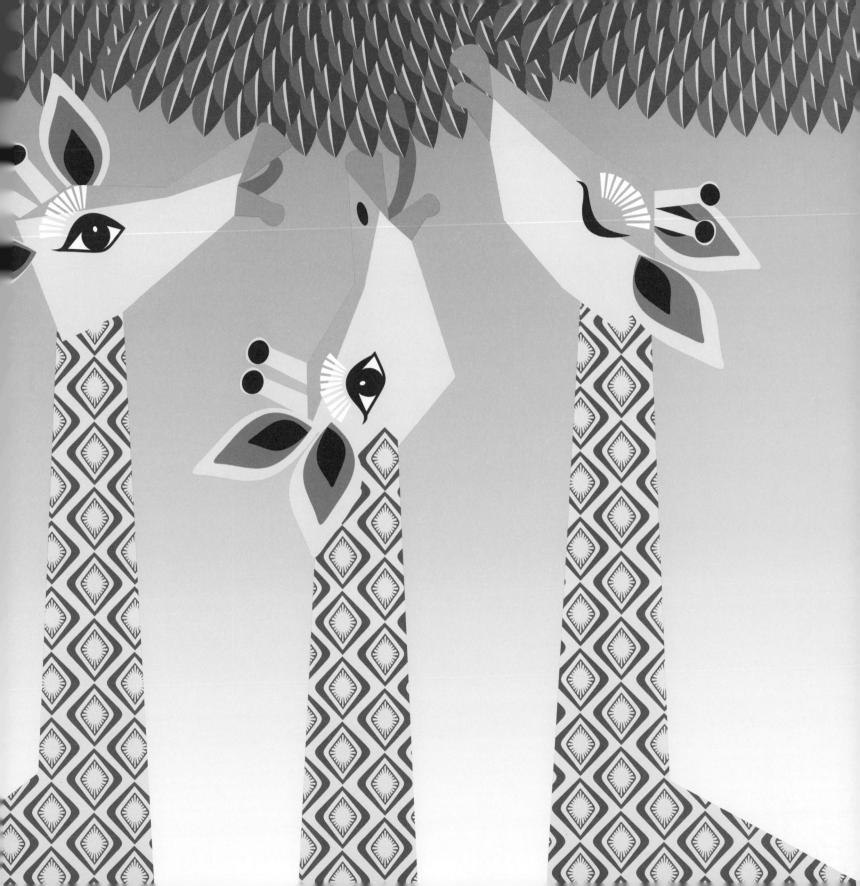

If you stood right next to one
you might just reach his knees.

Elephants are really smart,

with a super sense of smell.

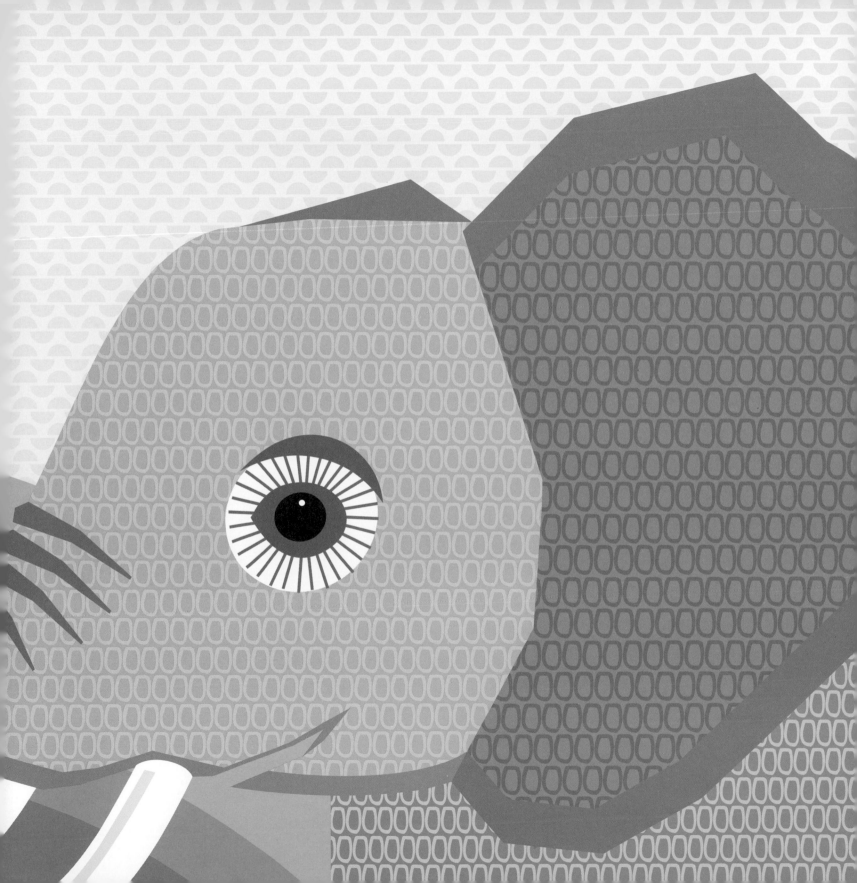

They like to care for relatives when they're not feeling well.

Zebras make a dazzling sight
as they go rushing by.

They all have such lovely stripes
but can you work out why?

Hippos love the water,
for hours and hours
they'll stand.

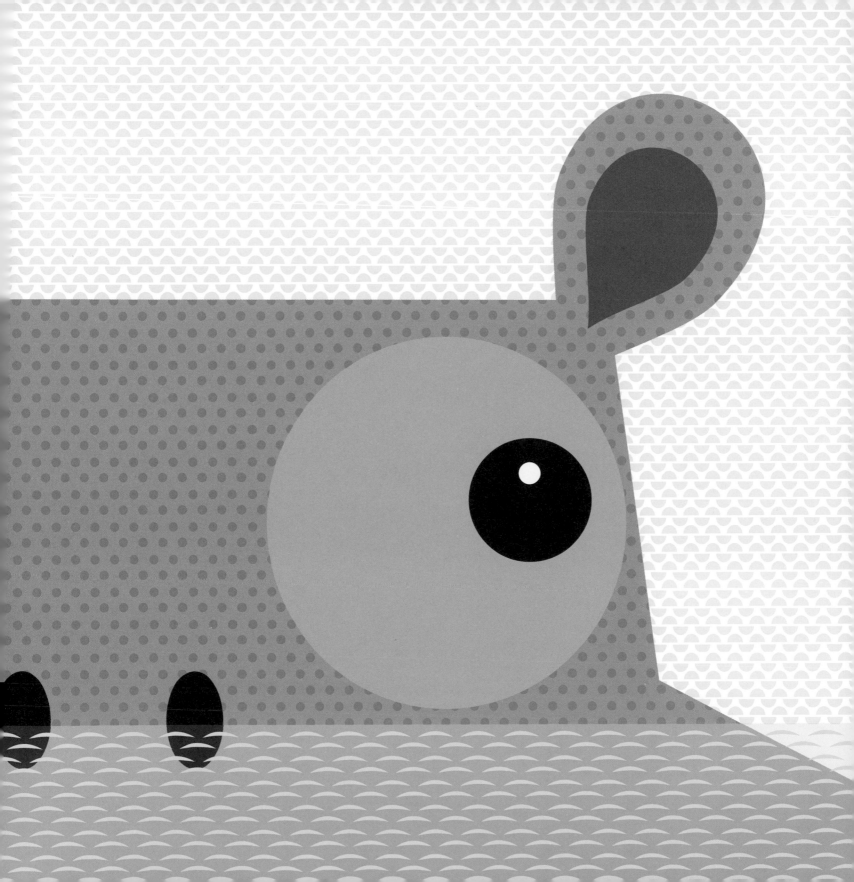

At night their tummies rumble
so they head back onto land.

Out on the savanna
it's getting even hotter.
Was it really fun to
be a safari wildlife
spotter?

First published 2015 by Button Books, an imprint of Guild of Master Craftsman Publications Ltd, Castle Place, 166 High Street, Lewes, East Sussex BN7 1XU, UK. Text, designs, and illustrations © Madeleine Rogers, 2015. Copyright in the Work © GMC Publications Ltd, 2015. ISBN 978 1 90898 531 6. Distributed by Publishers Group West in the United States. All rights reserved. The right of Madeleine Rogers to be identified as the author of this work has been asserted in accordance with the Copyright, Designs, and Patents Act 1988, sections 77 and 78. No part of this publication may be reproduced, stored in a retrieval system, or transmitted in any form or by any means without the prior permission of the publisher and copyright owner. This book is sold subject to the condition that all designs are copyright and are not for commercial reproduction without the permission of the designer and copyright owner. Whilst every effort has been made to obtain permission from the copyright holders for all material used in this book, the publishers will be pleased to hear from anyone who has not been appropriately acknowledged and to make the correction in future reprints. The publishers and author can accept no legal responsibility for any consequences arising from the application of information, advice, or instructions given in this publication. A catalog record for this book is available from the British Library. Color origination by GMC Reprographics. Printed in China.

FSC
www.fsc.org
MIX
Paper from
responsible sources
FSC® C020056